POSITIVELY POOH

A Book for Expotitions and New Adventures

EGMONT

We bring stories to life

First published in Great Britain 2005 by Egmont UK Limited
239 Kensington High Street, London W8 6SA

ISBN 978 1 4052 2047 7
ISBN 1 4052 2047 3

3 5 7 9 10 8 6 4 2

A CIP catalogue record for this title is available from the British Library

Printed and bound in Malaysia

POSITIVELY POOH

A Book for Expotitions and Adventures

A.A. Milne

Illustrated by E.H. Shepard

EGMONT

Be clear what exactly your Expotition will be

'We're all going on an Expotition with
    Christopher Robin!' [Pooh]
'What is it when we're on it?' [Rabbit]
  'A sort of boat, I think,' said Pooh.

'We are all going on an Expedition,' said Christopher Robin, as he got up and brushed himself. 'Thank you, Pooh.'

'Going on an Expotition?' said Pooh eagerly. 'I don't think I've ever been on one of those. Where are we going to on this Expotition?'

'Expedition, silly old Bear. It's got an "x" in it.'

'Oh!' said Pooh. 'I know.' But he didn't really.

'We're going to discover the North Pole.'

'Oh!' said Pooh again. 'What *is* the North Pole?' he asked.

'It's just a thing you discover,' said Christopher Robin carelessly, not being quite sure himself.

'Oh! I see,' said Pooh. 'Are bears any good at discovering it?'

'Of course they are.'

Be sure you know where your
Expotition will take you

Find the adventure that suits you

'Come on, Tigger,' he called out. 'It's easy.'
But Tigger was holding on to the branch and
saying to himself: 'It's all very well for Jumping
Animals like Kangas, but it's quite different for
Swimming Animals like Tiggers.' And he thought
of himself floating on his back down a river,
or striking out from one island to another, and
he felt that that was really the life for a Tigger.

Apply planning and forethought

'And I would go in after it,' said Pooh excitedly, 'only very carefully so as not to hurt myself, and I would get to the Jar of Honey, and I should lick round the edges first of all, pretending that there wasn't any more, you know, and then I should walk away and think about it a little, and then I should come back and start licking in the middle of the jar, and then –'

Know what you are
letting yourself in for

'There's just one thing,' said Piglet, fidgeting a bit. 'I was talking to Christopher Robin, and he said that a Kanga was Generally Regarded as One of the Fiercer Animals. I am not frightened of Fierce Animals in the ordinary way, but it is well known that if One of the Fiercer Animals is Deprived of Its Young, it becomes as fierce as Two of the Fiercer Animals. In which case "*Aha!*" is perhaps a *foolish* thing to say.'

Be ready for an Adventure about to happen!

Christopher Robin was sitting outside his door, putting on his Big Boots. As soon as he saw the Big Boots, Pooh knew that an Adventure was going to happen, and he brushed the honey off his nose with the back of his paw, and spruced himself up as well as he could, so as to look Ready for Anything.

Create a buzz before you go

He trotted along happily, and by-the-by he crossed the stream and came to the place where his friends-and-relations lived. There seemed to be even more of them about than usual this morning, and having nodded to a hedgehog or two, with whom he was too busy to shake hands and having said, 'Good morning, good morning,' importantly to some of the others, and 'Ah, there you are,' kindly, to the smaller ones, he waved a paw at them over his shoulder, and was gone; leaving such an air of excitement and I-don't-know-what behind him . . .

Visualise your success – and it will happen!

Pooh looked proud at being called a stout and helpful bear, and said modestly that he just happened to think of it. You tied a piece of string to Piglet, and you flew up to the letter-box, with the other end in your beak, and you pushed it through the wire and brought it down to the floor, and you and Pooh pulled hard at this end, and Piglet went slowly up at the other end. And there you were.

Put the steps of your plan in order

PLAN TO CAPTURE BABY ROO

1. *General Remarks*. Kanga runs faster than any of Us, even Me.
2. *More General Remarks*. Kanga never takes her eye off Baby Roo, except when he's safely buttoned up in her pocket.
3. *Therefore*. If we are to capture Baby Roo, we must

get a Long Start, because Kanga runs faster than any of Us, even Me. (See 1.)

4. *A Thought.* If Roo had jumped out of Kanga's pocket and Piglet had jumped in, Kanga wouldn't know the difference, because Piglet is a Very Small Animal.
5. Like Roo.
6. But Kanga would have to be looking the other way first, so as not to see Piglet jumping in.
7. See 2.
8. *Another Thought.* But if Pooh was talking to her very excitedly, she might look the other way for a moment.
9. And then I could run away with Roo.
10. Quickly.
11. *And Kanga wouldn't discover the difference until Afterwards.*

Try to remember your previous steps

'That's funny,' he thought. 'I know I had a jar of honey there. A full jar, full of honey right up to the top, and it had HUNNY written on it, so that I should know it was honey. That's very funny.' And then he began to wander up and down, wondering where it was and murmuring a murmur to himself. Like this:

It's very, very funny
'Cos I *know* I had some honey;
'Cos it had a label on,
Saying HUNNY.

A goloptious full-up pot too,
And I don't know where it's got to,
No, I don't know where it's gone –
Well, it's funny.

He had murmured this to himself three times
in a singing sort of way, when suddenly
he remembered. He had put it into the
Cunning Trap to catch the Heffalump.
'Bother!' said Pooh.

Be positive about
meeting new people

'Hallo, Eeyore!' said Pooh. 'This is Tigger.'

'What is?' said Eeyore.

'This,' explained Pooh and Piglet together, and Tigger smiled his happiest smile and said nothing. Eeyore walked all round Tigger one way, and then turned and walked all round him the other way.

'What did you say it was?' he asked.

'Tigger.'

'Ah!' said Eeyore.

'He's just come,' explained Piglet.

'Ah!' said Eeyore again.

He thought for a long time and then said:

'When is he going?'

Take provisions!

'You'd better tell the others to get ready . . .
And we must all bring Provisions.' [said
Christopher Robin]
'Bring what?'
'Things to eat.'
'Oh!' said Pooh happily. 'I thought you said
Provisions . . .'

Helping your friends is an Adventure!

Pooh felt that he ought to say something helpful
about it, but didn't quite know what. So he
decided to do something helpful instead.
'Eeyore,' he said solemnly, 'I, Winnie-the-Pooh,
will find your tail for you.'
'Thank you, Pooh,' answered Eeyore. 'You're a
real friend,' said he. 'Not Like Some,' he said.
So Winnie-the-Pooh went off to find Eeyore's tail.

Be thorough

Winnie-the-Pooh read the two notices very carefully, first from left to right, and afterwards, in case he had missed some of it, from right to left. Then, to make quite sure, he knocked and pulled the knocker, and he pulled and knocked the bell-rope, and he called out in a very loud voice, 'Owl! I require an answer! It's Bear speaking.'

Be open to new ideas

'I've been finding things in the Forest,' said Tigger importantly. 'I've found a pooh and a piglet and an eeyore, but I can't find any breakfast.' . . . Kanga said very kindly, 'Well, look in my cupboard, Tigger dear, and see what you'd like.' . . . But the more Tigger put his nose into this and his paw into that, the more things he found which Tiggers didn't like . . . he leant over the back of Roo's chair, and suddenly he put out his tongue, and took one large galollop, and . . . the Extract of Malt had gone . . . Then Tigger looked up at the ceiling, and closed his eyes, and his tongue went round and round his chops, in case he had left any outside, and a peaceful smile came over his face as he said, 'So *that's* what Tiggers like!'

'Ho-*ho*!' said Christopher Robin loudly and suddenly.
Piglet jumped six inches in the air with Surprise
and Anxiety, but Pooh went on dreaming.
'It's the Heffalump!' thought Piglet nervously.
'Now, then!' He hummed in his throat a little,
so that none of the words should stick, and then,
in the most delightfully easy way, he said:
'Tra-la-la, tra-la-la,' as if he had just thought of it.
But he didn't look round, because if you look
round and see a Very Fierce Heffalump looking
down at you, sometimes you forget what you
were going to say.

Sometimes you have to be
brave, like Piglet

Prepare by imagining the scenario

[Piglet] knew just what he would say:

HEFFALUMP (*gloatingly*): 'Ho-ho!'

PIGLET (*carelessly*): 'Tra-la la, tra-la la.'

HEFFALUMP (*surprised, and not quite so sure of himself*): 'Ho-ho!'

PIGLET (*more carelessly still*): 'Tiddle-um-tum, tiddle-um-tum.'

HEFFALUMP (*beginning to say Ho-ho and turning it awkwardly into a cough*): 'H'r'm! What's all this?'

PIGLET (*surprised*): 'Hallo! This is a trap I've made and I'm waiting for a Heffalump to fall into it.'

HEFFALUMP (*greatly disappointed*): 'Oh!'
(*After a long silence*): 'Are you sure?'
PIGLET: 'Yes.'
HEFFALUMP: 'Oh!' (*nervously*): 'I – I thought it
was a trap I'd made to catch Piglets.'
PIGLET (*surprised*): 'Oh, no!'
HEFFALUMP: 'Oh!' (*apologetically*): 'I – I must
have got it wrong then.'
PIGLET: 'I'm afraid so.' (*politely*)

Be inventive when you're
in a tight spot

Then he had an idea, and I think that
for a Bear of Very Little Brain, it was
a good idea. He said to himself:
'If a bottle can float, then a jar can float,
and if a jar floats, I can sit on the top
of it, if it's a very big jar.'

'The thing to do is as follows. First, Issue a Reward. Then –'

'Just a moment,' said Pooh, holding up his paw. '*What* do we do to this – what you were saying? You sneezed just as you were going to tell me.'

'I *didn't* sneeze.'

'Yes, you did, Owl.'

'Excuse me, Pooh, I didn't. You can't sneeze without knowing it.'

'Well, you can't know it without something having been sneezed.'

'What I *said* was, "First *Issue* a Reward".'

'You're doing it again,' said Pooh sadly.

'A Reward!' said Owl very loudly. 'We write a notice to say that we will give a large something to anybody who finds Eeyore's tail.'

Persist, even if others don't understand you

Look on the bright side

'I shouldn't be surprised if it hailed a good
deal to-morrow,' Eeyore was saying.
'Blizzards and what-not. Being fine to-day
doesn't Mean Anything.'

'I'm giving this to Eeyore,' he explained,
'as a present. What are *you* going to give?'
'Couldn't I give it too?' said Piglet.
'From both of us?'
'No,' said Pooh. 'That would *not* be a
good plan.'

'It's a nice pot,' said Owl, looking at it all round.
'Couldn't I give it too? From both of us?'
'No,' said Pooh. 'That would *not* be a good
plan. Now I'll just wash it first, and then you
can write on it.'

Always be assertive . . .

...but know when to
exercise caution

'Hush!' said Christopher Robin, turning round to Pooh, 'we're just coming to a Dangerous Place.'

'It's a little Anxious,' he said to himself, 'to be a Very Small Animal Entirely Surrounded by Water. Christopher Robin and Pooh could escape by Climbing Trees, and Kanga could escape by Jumping, and Rabbit could escape by Burrowing, and Owl could escape by Flying, and Eeyore could escape by – by Making a Loud Noise Until Rescued, and here am I, surrounded by water and I can't do *anything*.

. . . .

Then suddenly he remembered a story which Christopher Robin had told him about a man on a desert island who had written something in a bottle and thrown it into the sea; and Piglet thought that if he wrote something in a bottle and threw it in the water, perhaps somebody would come and rescue *him*!

Don't give up, even if you
think you're stuck

Trust your instincts

'Now then, Piglet, let's go home.'
'But, Pooh,' cried Piglet, all excited,
'do you know the way?'
'No,' said Pooh. 'But there are twelve pots
of honey in my cupboard, and they've been
calling to me for hours. I couldn't hear them
properly before because Rabbit *would* talk,
but if nobody says anything except those
twelve pots, I *think*, Piglet, I shall know
where they're coming from. Come on.'

And he gave a deep sigh, and tried very hard to listen to what Owl was saying. But Owl went on and on, using longer and longer words, until at last he came back to where he started, and he explained that the person to write out this notice was Christopher Robin. 'It was he who wrote the ones on my front door for me. Did you see them, Pooh?'

For some time now Pooh had been saying 'Yes' and 'No' in turn, with his eyes shut, to all that Owl was saying, and having said, 'Yes, yes,' last time, he said, 'No, not at all,' now, without really knowing what Owl was talking about.

Avoid misunderstandings –
learn to communicate

Keep everyone up to date with your progress

And two days later Rabbit happened to meet
Eeyore in the Forest.
'Hallo, Eeyore,' he said, 'what are *you* looking for?'
'Small, of course,' said Eeyore. 'Haven't you
any brain?'
'Oh, but didn't I tell you?' said Rabbit.
'Small was found two days ago.'
There was a moment's silence. 'Ha-ha,' said
Eeyore bitterly. 'Merriment and what-not.
Don't apologise. It's just what *would* happen.'

Think long-term

'What are you doing?'
'I'm planting a haycorn, Pooh, so that it can grow
up into an oak-tree, and have lots of haycorns just
outside the front door instead of having to walk
miles and miles, do you see, Pooh?'

You may get where you're
going in a roundabout way

'Pooh,' he said, 'where did you find that pole?'
Pooh looked at the pole in his hands.
'I just found it,' he said. 'I thought it ought
to be useful. I just picked it up.'
'Pooh,' said Christopher Robin solemnly, 'the
Expedition is over. You have found the North Pole!'
'Oh!' said Pooh.

Piglet felt much better after this, and when everything was ready, and he found himself slowly going up to the ceiling, he was so proud that he would have called out 'Look at *me*!' if he hadn't been afraid that Pooh and Owl would let go of their end of the string and look at him.

Be proud of yourself when
you've done a Grand Thing

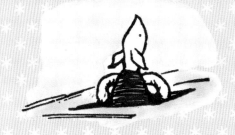

Reward yourself after each Expotition and Adventure!

They stuck the pole in the ground, and
Christopher Robin tied a message on to it:
North Pole Discovered By Pooh
Pooh Found It
Then they all went home again. And I think,
but I am not quite sure, that Roo had a hot
bath and went straight to bed. But Pooh went
back to his own house, and feeling very proud
of what he had done, had a little something
to revive himself.